Are you scared of thunder?

Curious Questions & answers about...

Weather

Where do you live on planet Earth?

Do you prefer hot or cold weather?

Where would you go on an adventure?

What name would you give to a hurricane?

What do you do to have fun?

Words by Philip Steele
Illustrations by Mike Moran

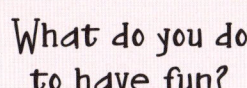

Little Hippo Books

What is weather?

Earth is surrounded by a layer of air called the atmosphere. The way the atmosphere behaves is always changing. It is these changes that give us the weather, which may be hot, cold, wet, windy, or sunny.

Sun

Be careful the wind doesn't blow your hat off!

Earth

The atmosphere is filled with moving air and clouds

Why does weather happen?

The Sun is the nearest star to Earth. It is far, far away in space, but its incredible heat warms our planet. This warmth affects the way that air presses against Earth's surface. Differences between cold and warm places create strong winds, as well as currents in the oceans.

South Pole

Why do seasons change?

As Earth travels around the Sun, it is tilted. This means that northern and southern parts lean toward to the Sun at different times of the year. So when the north part is leaning toward the Sun it is summer there, and winter in the southern part.

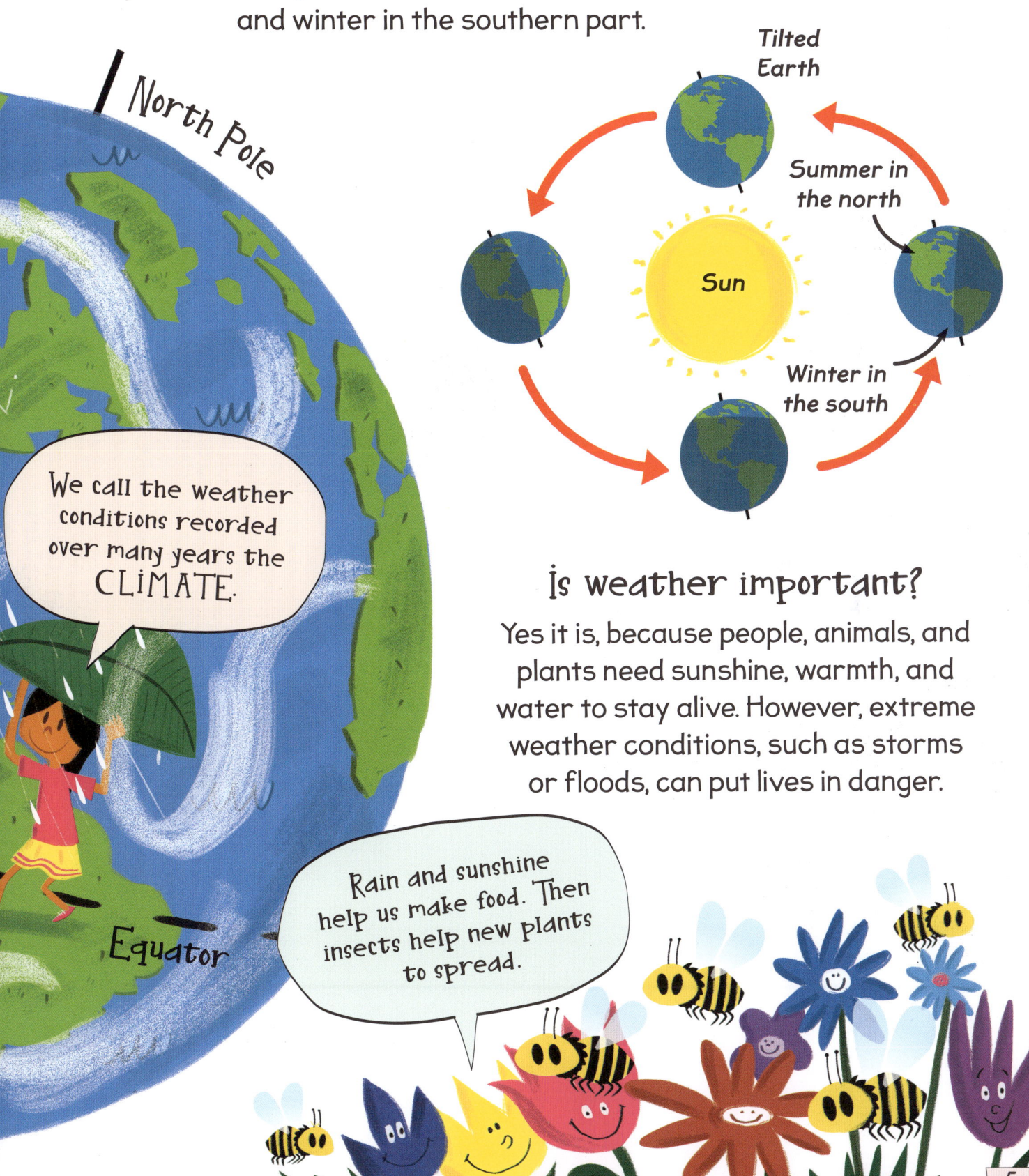

We call the weather conditions recorded over many years the CLIMATE.

Is weather important?

Yes it is, because people, animals, and plants need sunshine, warmth, and water to stay alive. However, extreme weather conditions, such as storms or floods, can put lives in danger.

Rain and sunshine help us make food. Then insects help new plants to spread.

What makes water wonderful?

"Water is a liquid. It can freeze to become solid ice. It can turn into a gas called water vapor. Water may change its form, but it lasts forever."

2 It gets gassy

Heat from the Sun turns water into a gas, called water vapor. This is **evaporation**.

1 There's lots of it!

Over **two thirds** of the Earth's surface is covered in water.

Water is precious

Fresh water keeps us **alive**. Water helps plants grow, too. We can wash in it, swim in it, sail on it, drink it, and play in it!

Whoosh! Splash!

3 It rises and cools

As warm water vapor rises, it cools down. It **condenses**, turning back into liquid.

The higher you go, the colder it gets!

4 It makes clouds

Water droplets or solid ice crystals gather around specks of dust and form **clouds**.

5 It falls back down

Don't forget your umbrella!

Water droplets or ice crystals form **raindrops** or **snowflakes**, which fall back to Earth.

6 It goes on and on

Rain and melted snow fill rivers, lakes, and oceans, then the whole **water cycle** starts all over again. It helps create our weather.

How hot does it get?

In California's Death Valley, the top temperature ever recorded was over 132°F. A weather satellite has recorded over 158°F in the Lut Desert in Iran.

Where is the driest place on Earth?

The Atacama Desert in Chile. Once, no rain fell there for over 14 years. Long periods without rain are called droughts.

We can measure temperature in degrees Fahrenheit (°F). At the center of the Sun it's about 27 million°F.

Why do lizards sunbathe?

Reptiles such as lizards are cold-blooded, which means that they can't make their own heat. They bask in the sunshine to warm themselves up.

Atacama Desert

Lizard

How can plants survive in a desert?

Some plants have their own water supply. Cacti store water in their thick, spiky stems. Baobab trees store water inside their big, fat trunks.

Cactus

Baobab tree

Why can the Sun be a danger?

The Sun can burn your skin and make you sick. On a sunny day, cover up your skin, wear a hat, slap on some sunscreen, and drink plenty of water.

Don't forget I need a drink too!

Where does the weather happen?

In the layer of the atmosphere that is closest to Earth's surface. The atmosphere surrounds our planet like a giant blanket, screening out some harmful rays that come from the Sun.

Atmosphere

Cumulonimbus

What is a weather system?

Huge masses of air that swirl over Earth's surface are called weather systems. High pressure systems press air down against the land. They bring drier, clearer weather. Low pressure systems bring mild or rainy weather. The border between two systems is called a front.

On TV, the weather is explained with maps and symbols.

Cirrus

Why do clouds have funny shapes?

Some clouds are white and puffy, some are thin and streaky. Some pile up like big dark towers, some form little blobs. Their shape depends on whether they are full of water droplets or ice crystals and how high up they are.

Mackerel sky

Some clouds look like dragons, castles, or bears in the sky. What can you see up there?

Is there a pot of gold at the end of a rainbow?

Only in fairy tales! Rainbows are the most beautiful sights in the sky. Air has no color, but when sunlight passes through rain or mist, the water droplets break up the light into an arc of shimmering colors.

Why does the wind blow?

Because as warm air rises, cold air whooshes in to take its place, and the wind blows! Some winds blow between land and sea. Some cross deserts and mountains. Others blow all the way around the planet.

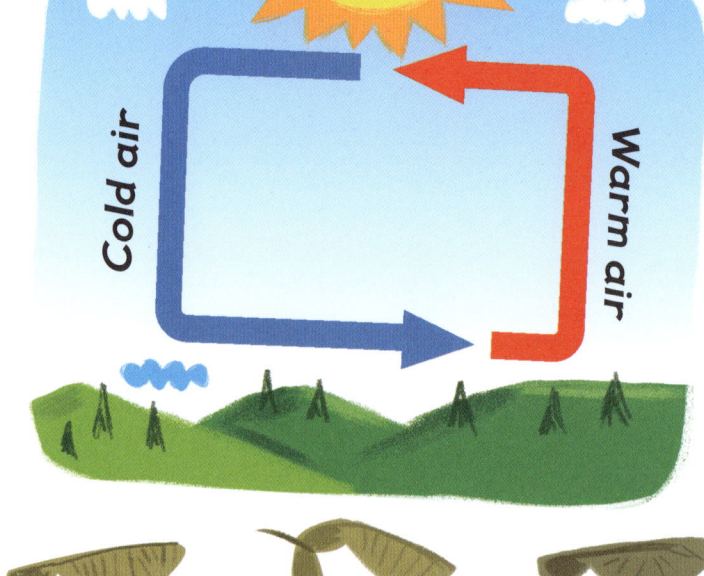

Sycamore seeds

How does the wind help plants?

Many trees and flowering plants have seeds that are scattered by the wind. Dandelion seeds are light and fluffy, and float a long way. Sycamore seeds are like helicopter blades, spinning around.

Dandelion seeds

What is a monsoon?

It is a wind that blows across India. The winter monsoon brings dry weather. In summer it picks up lots of water from the ocean and brings heavy rains to the dry land.

Summer monsoon can bring flooding.

Wandering albatross

Why do birds ride on the wind?

Condor

So we can fly long distances without too much flapping. Over the Southern Ocean, albatrosses like me glide on powerful winds. In South America, condors use currents of warm air to soar above mountains.

Pillar

How do winds shape rock?

Winds often carry dust, grit, or sand. They blast rocks and cliffs, wearing them down into all sorts of shapes. Water, ice, and heat also shape the surface of planet Earth.

Arch

What is a hurricane?

It's a terrifying tropical storm, also called a typhoon or a cyclone. A great storm cloud spins around as it sweeps over the ocean. Hurricane-force winds can reach 110 miles an hour or even more.

The calm center is called the "eye" of the storm.

Is it deadly?

When a hurricane smashes into land it can be deadly. There are huge waves, heavy rain, floods, and mudslides. Trees can be blown over, homes may be destroyed, and lives may be at risk.

Why are thunder clouds dark?

Thunder clouds are so full of water droplets that they look very dark. They tower up to 9 miles high.

How do clouds make lightning?

Water vapor rushes up into clouds from the warm ground. Once inside, the vapor cools and freezes, forming balls of ice called hailstones. Air currents ping these up and down inside the cloud, making an electric charge.

> In a thunderstorm, stay away from water or metal fences.

Did you know?

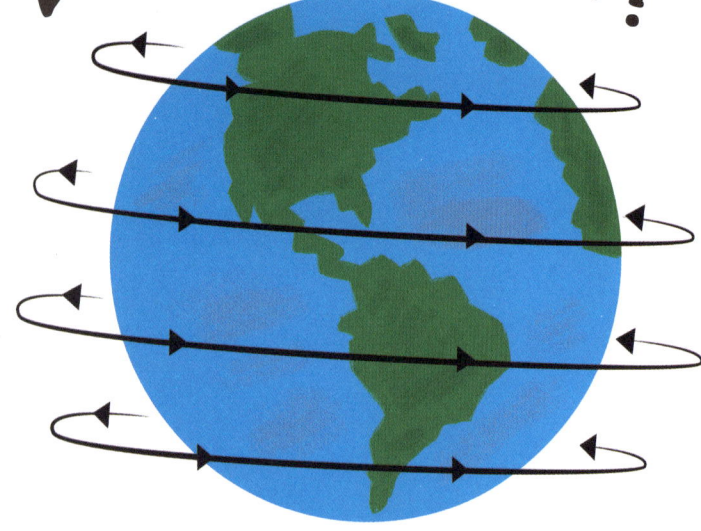

Super-powerful long-distance winds called **jet streams** rip along about 6.2 miles above the Earth's surface.

The Inuit people of the Arctic can build **igloos**—overnight shelters made from blocks of frozen snow. These are actually quite cozy!

It is said that no two **snowflakes** have exactly the same design!

Fog is just a low-level cloud. The Grand Banks off Newfoundland, Canada, have about 206 foggy days each year.

As you are reading these words, there are about 2,000 **thunderstorms** happening around the world.

The spinning of the Earth forces **winds** that blow from the Poles to the Equator to change direction.

COUGH!
When fumes from cars and factories react with sunlight, the air is filled with horrible, poisonous **smog**.

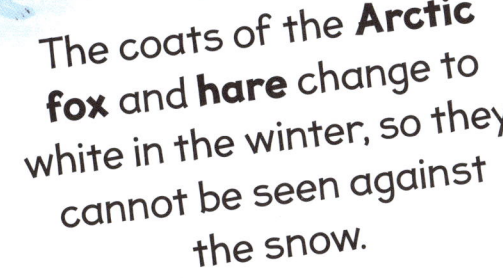

The coats of the **Arctic fox** and **hare** change to white in the winter, so they cannot be seen against the snow.

Fir trees have thin, tough leaves called **needles**, which stay on all winter. These help capture sunlight all year round. They can store water and survive harsh winter storms.

Long ago, people believed that the weather was controlled **by gods and goddesses**. Inti was the Inca Sun god. Thor was the Norse god of thunder.

How are snowflakes formed?

When water droplets freeze around specks of dust in a cloud, snowflakes form. These ice crystals freeze more droplets, building up amazing starry shapes and patterns. They stick together to make bigger flakes.

Snowflakes have SIX sides, or points.

What is a blizzard?

A blizzard is a heavy snow storm driven by high winds. Snow piles up in deep drifts. It's hard to see where you are going as everything looks white!

Why are mountaintops snowy?
Mountaintops are often covered in snow, even in hot countries. The higher you climb, the more the air expands and cools. This leads to more moisture—and snowy mountain conditions.

Where does frost make flowers?
On cold surfaces such as windows, ice, or rock. Ice crystals spread into beautiful patterns, which look like ferns or flowers.

Does the sea ever freeze?
Yes it does, but because the sea contains salt, it has a lower freezing point. It turns to ice below -35.6° Fahrenheit. Freshwater rivers and lakes freeze at 32° Fahrenheit.

DANGER THIN ICE!

How many?

331 — The number of days it once rained nonstop on the Hawaiian Island of Oahu!

4,000 — The number of hours of sunshine that Yuma, Arizona, U.S. receives in a year. It may be the sunniest place on Earth!

The biggest tropical storm ever recorded was a typhoon named Tip, in 1979. It measured **1,379** miles across.

5 years! That's how long a water-holding frog can go without water during a drought!

37.7 feet: The depth of snowfall at Tamarack in California, U.S., in March 1911.

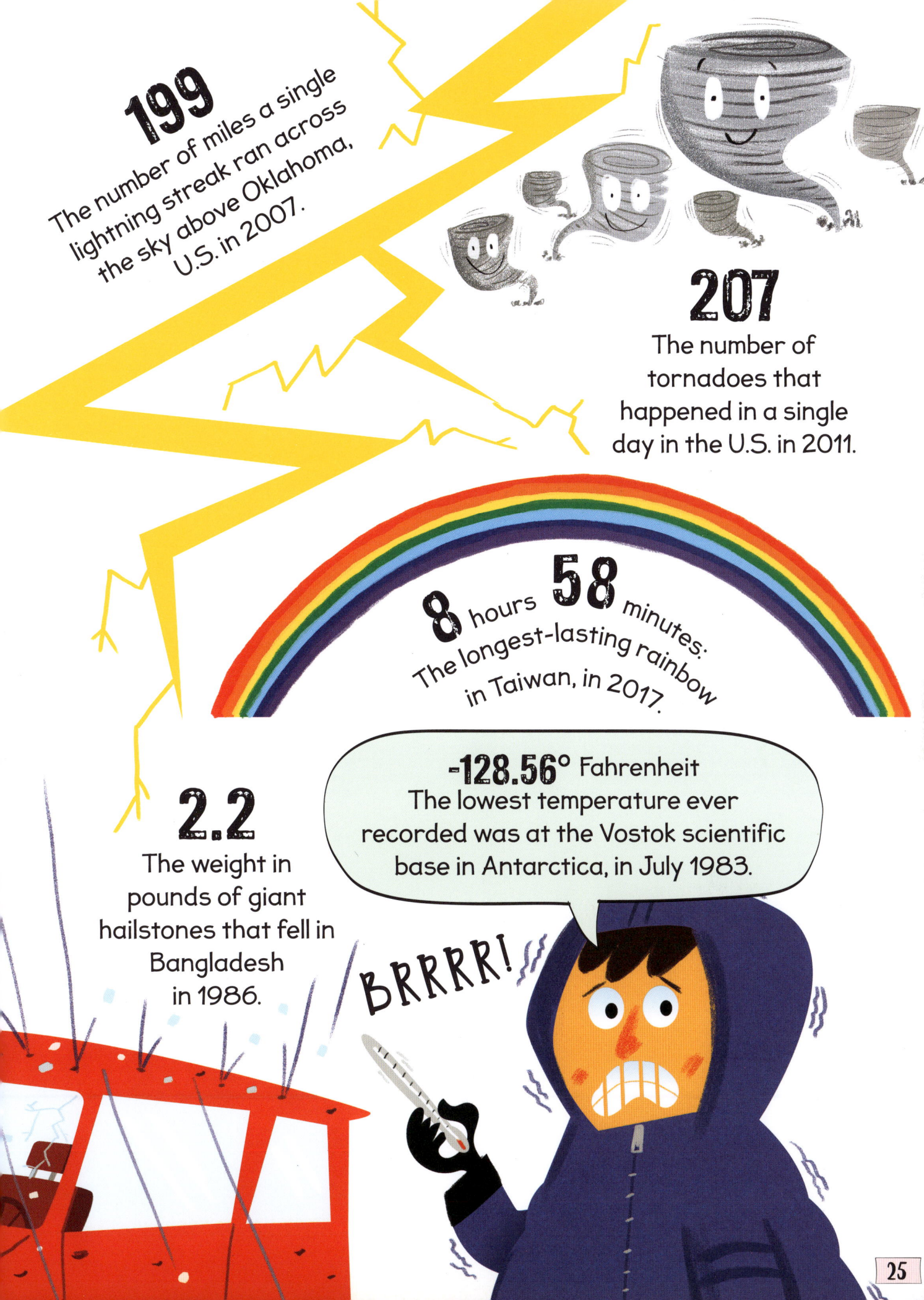

How do we measure the weather?

All sorts of clever gadgets have been invented over the years to measure how the weather behaves. Today, the numbers are often recorded and displayed digitally.

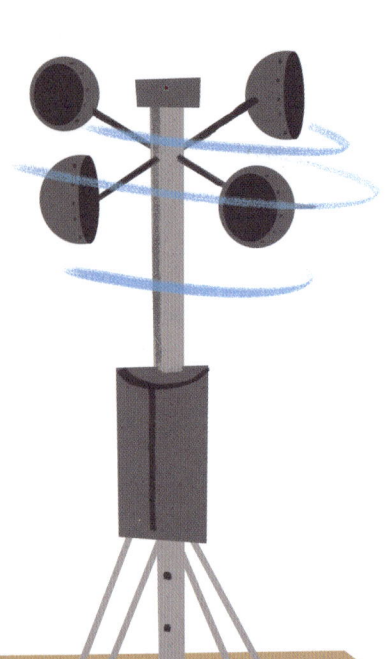

Anemometers measure wind speed. They are often fixed to tall buildings, bridges, and ships.

Rain gauges collect and measure the amount of rain that falls into a jar.

Thermometers measure how hot or cold it gets. The best known thermometers show how a liquid metal called mercury goes up or down inside a glass tube. Most weather scientists today use electrical resistance thermometers.

Does the climate ever change?

Over millions of years, Earth's climate has gone through many changes. In the past there have been great ice ages, when ice spread out from the poles.

I lived in the ice age thousands of years ago.

Woolly mammoth

What's happening today?

The climate is changing very quickly. This is because we are cutting down forests and burning too much oil, gas, and coal. We are filling the atmosphere with gases that make the planet overheat.

Solar panels use energy from the Sun to create electricity.

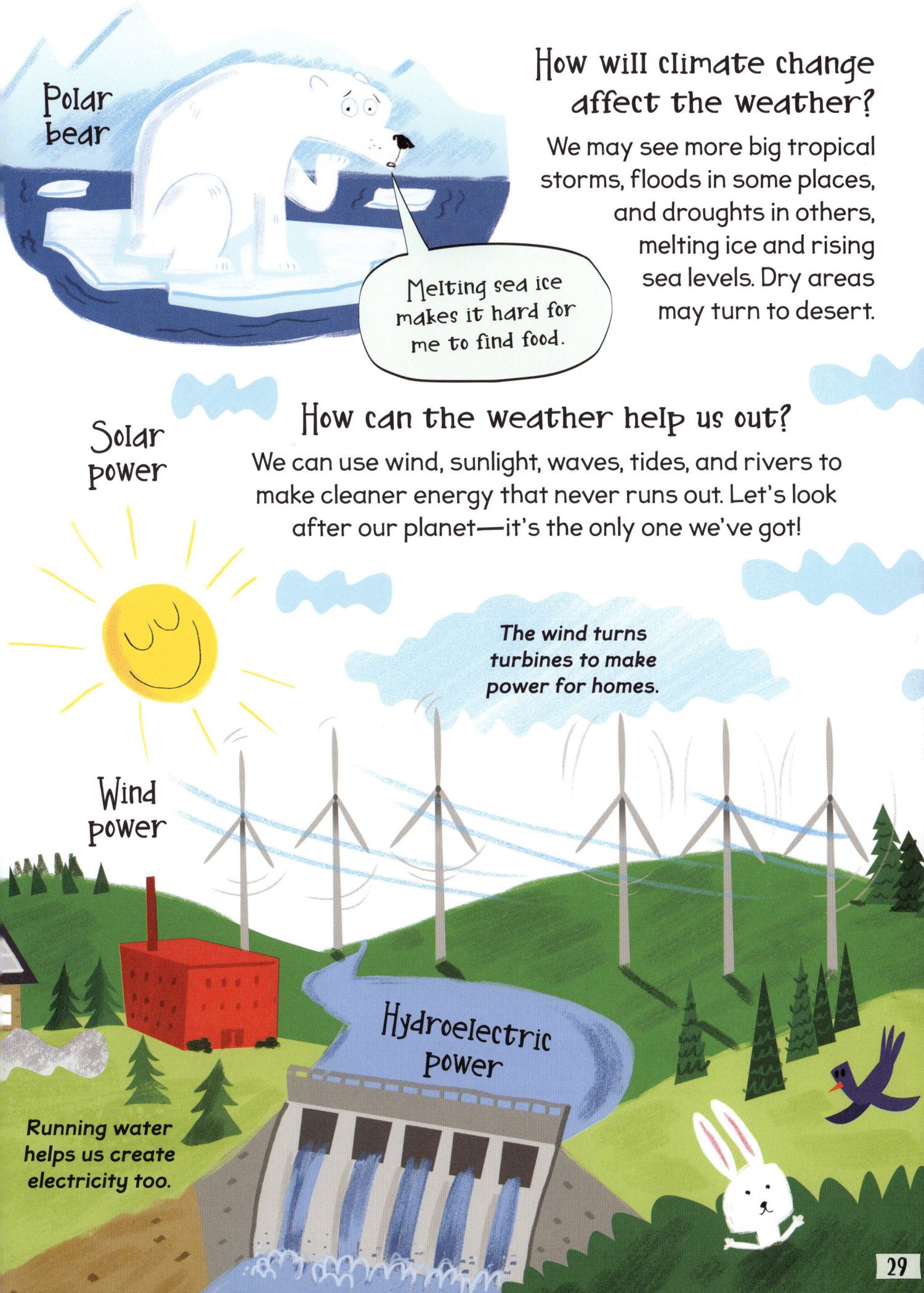

A compendium of questions

Why is rain sometimes red?

If rain gets mixed with sand picked up by desert winds, it can be red or orange.

Why are hurricanes given names?

It's an easy way of remembering which was which. Famous tropical storms have been called Katrina, Maria, Mitch, and David.

Why do crocodiles like tropical storms?

If it floods, crocodiles can go hunting in the high street. You'd better watch out!

Where is there a special snow festival?

It is held each year in Sapporo, Japan. People make amazing statues and sculptures from ice and snow.

Why do people build houses on stilts?

When it floods in the rainy season in Assam, India, the houses stay high and dry.